CW00840615

BUSES IN
OUTER LONDON
SINCE 1990

BUSES IN
OUTER LONDON
SINCE 1990

DAVID MOTH

AMBERLEY

First published 2019

Amberley Publishing
The Hill, Stroud
Gloucestershire, GL5 4EP

www.amberley-books.com

Copyright © David Moth, 2019

The right of David Moth to be identified as
the Author of this work has been asserted in
accordance with the Copyrights, Designs and
Patents Act 1988.

ISBN 978 1 4456 8784 1 (print)
ISBN 978 1 4456 8785 8 (ebook)

All rights reserved. No part of this book may be
reprinted or reproduced or utilised in any form
or by any electronic, mechanical or other means,
now known or hereafter invented, including
photocopying and recording, or in any information
storage or retrieval system, without the permission
in writing from the Publishers.

British Library Cataloguing in Publication Data.
A catalogue record for this book is available from
the British Library.

Origination by Amberley Publishing.
Printed in the UK.

Introduction

Most photo collections of London to tend to favour central London to a large degree. After all, that is where the best known parts of London are, and indeed where the Routemasters were during the period covered by this book (1990 to 2015). The premise of this book was that I would strictly adhere to what is considered to be considered the statutory outer London boroughs, so as not to include any bus images at all from the inner London boroughs. Thus there are no images taken in Streatham, Camden, Holloway, Putney, etc.

Although I am aware of a few books which concentrate on buses in East London, a few of which I own myself, as far as I'm aware this is the first time someone has published a collection encompassing all of outer London (well, apart from Croydon, which I'm the first to admit is conspicuous by its absence from this book, probably more than any other outer London location).

Fans of Routemasters will not be entirely disappointed as there are a small number of photos of Routemasters taken in Willesden.

There are 179 images in this book, of which 177 were taken by myself, with the other two taken by a friend of mine on a day out we had together in east and north London in 2013. It just happened that he had a camera with him that day while I was 'between cameras' as I did have a tendency to drop mine. He took several photos that day, including one where I was clearly visible in the image, looking at the bus in Claybury Broadway, just north of Ilford. I have decided not to include that image as I didn't wish to inflict my rotund frame and bald patch on any readers of this book. He has given his consent to use images taken by him on that day out and I have fully credited him in those images.

There are four images in this book taken outside of Greater London, including one of London United Dennis Dart DT1 taken literally just yards outside of Greater London at Hampton Court station. The other three are of a Stagecoach Dennis Trident on the 96 at Bluewater, a Metrobus Scania CN94

Omnicity in Epsom on the 293 and a First Dennis Dart seen at Shenfield on rail replacement. Although that last one was some way inside Essex, I felt inclusion was justified as the vehicle in question was normally used on the 193 in the Romford area at the time.

As is the case for my previous photo collections, the photos were taken by me over quite a long period of time (in this case twenty-five years) for my own enjoyment as a record of the ever-changing bus scene. I am not a professional photographer by any stretch of the imagination and I was generally using the best camera I could afford at the time. The vast majority of photos in this book were taken with film cameras, generally using 100 speed films in the summer and 400 speed during the rest of the year. All images from 2010 onwards were taken with digital cameras (I was using film cameras up until late 2009, something I now acknowledge to be a mistake).

There is almost inevitably a bit of a bias towards certain areas at the expense of others, simply because of the places I tended to gravitate towards. Hounslow and Kingston are very strongly represented, mainly due to me having friends in those areas, while there are no Croydon images. And being based in Essex, then Cambridgeshire, then back to Essex during the time period of these photos, there are a large amount of East London images, especially Romford, mainly because these were the easier to access areas of London for me. Although in common with a lot of other 'bus cranks', I did tend to consider the bus scene in Romford of particular interest, especially in the 1990s.

While inevitably not everyone's favourite locations, vehicle types or operators will feature in this book, I have tried my best to include an eclectic selection from outer London during this time. I have generally arranged the photos in a geographic order, starting with Bluewater and sweeping around London clockwise to take in Morden, Wimbledon, Kingston, Hounslow, Uxbridge, etc., ending up in east London with plenty taken in Chingford, Tottenham, Barking, Romford, etc.

I do hope people enjoy what has been a labour of love and apologies to anyone whose favourite area or operator may have been missed out.

David M. Moth
June 2018

Selkent Leyland Titan T1003 (A603 THV), seen at Bromley North station on Wednesday 31 August 1994. Behind is a Kentish Bus Dennis Dart with Northern Counties bodywork.

Kentish Bus Leyland Atlantean 685 (KPJ 275W) is seen briefly resting at Bromley North station on 31 August 1994 having just arrived on the lengthy 402 from Tunbridge Wells before returning to that famous Kentish town via Sevenoaks.

Stagecoach Selkent Dennis Trident X267 NNO is seen on 5 December 2000 at one of the outermost extremities of the TfL bus network, i.e. Bluewater shopping centre. Interestingly, the bus seems to be completely devoid of any fleetname, legal lettering or fleetnumber. This bus saw further service with Centrebus and Yorkshire Tiger.

Arriva South London M863 (OJD 863Y) is seen, looking very unloved, in Croydon in February 2000 on the 466 route, which was introduced in 1998 to replace parts of the 400 and 166. Metrobuses were taken off the 466 soon after I took this photo.

London General Metrobus M303 (BYX 303V) is seen opposite Morden Underground station on the 93 to Putney Bridge on Sunday 13 March 1994.

London General Leyland Fleetline DMS2368 (OJD 368R) is seen at the North Cheam terminus of the 93 on Thursday 24 October 1991. The 93 was one of the last trunk routes in London operated by Fleetlines, although they were gradually ousted from the route by Metrobuses in 1992.

When the various divisions of London Buses were privatised in 1994, London General was the subject of a management buyout. MCW Metrobus Mk 1 M144 (BYX 144V) is seen in Wimbledon on Friday 14 March 1996 in the attractive livery adopted by the company.

When Westlink was awarded the tender to operate the 131 in 1991, it acquired a small fleet of Leyland Titans to use on the route. It was unusual to see Titans on a south-west London route and they certainly stood out among what was still very much a plethora of Metrobuses at the time. The distinctive livery also helped. This is Wimbledon on Sunday 20 October 1991.

The 93 from Putney Bridge to North Cheam was still being operated by B20 type Leyland Fleetlines when I took this photo. London General DMS2288 (THX 288S) is seen at Wimbledon Common on Sunday 20 October 1991. London Buses would withdraw its last Fleetlines the following year.

London United Dennis Dart DT1 (G501 VYE) is seen at Hampton Court railway station, just outside Greater London by a matter of yards, on Sunday 29 March 1992. Numerically, this was the first of many Dennis Darts delivered to London Buses. This bus is now preserved.

London United Metrobus M1025 (A725 THV) is seen in Tolworth on the 281 to Hounslow on 27 April 1997. The 281 was identified by London Transport in the late 1970s as a possible route to use second-hand Routemasters new to Northern General on, had the forward-entrance buses been in suitable condition for LT to make use of them.

London United Metrobus M1015 (A715 THV) is seen on layover at Kingston bus station on Monday 4 September 2000. This was generally considered the most attractive of the various liveries adopted by the privatised former London Buses companies.

Transdev London United Dennis Trident TA336 (SN03 EBG) is captured in Kingston town centre on the 281 on Saturday 23 August 2008.

London & Country Dennis Dominator 605 (F605 RPG) is seen in the spring sunshine at Kingston bus station. Despite the presence of an LRT route sticker on the front of the bus, it is about to head off to Bookham on the lengthy commercially operated 479 on 30 May 1998.

Metrobus was taken over by the Go Ahead Group in 1999. On Sunday 26 October 2014, Scania CN94 Omnicity 566 (YN08 OAY) is seen in Epsom on the 293 TfL route to Morden. Alongside is preserved former London Transport AEC Regent RT 4779 (OLD 566).

Also taken on 26 October 2014 is this picture of Epsom Coaches Group Dennis Enviro 400 SL14 LNG in Kingston-upon-Thames. Alongside is preserved London Transport AEC Regent RT1700 (KYY 527).

MacNamara (Country Bus & Coach) former London United Metrobus B262 WUL is seen on rail replacement work at Hounslow railway station on Sunday 5 February 2006. This bus was new to London Buses as M1262.

London United Metrobus M825 (OJD 825Y) is seen at Heathrow Airport bus station on the 140 to Harrow Weald on Wednesday 5 February 1992.

London United Leyland Olympian L303 (G303 UYK) rests at the Lower Feltham terminus, where short workings of the 237 terminated, on Saturday 11 December 1993.

London United Leyland Olympian L310 (G310 UYK) is seen in Feltham town centre in the late autumn sunshine of Saturday 11 December 1993.

One of a batch of twenty-three single-door, all-Leyland Olympians purchased by London Buses for the 237, London United Leyland Olympian L293 (G293 UYK) is seen at the Minimax between Hounslow and Feltham on Saturday 7 December 1991.

Transdev London United Dennis Dart SN51 SXX passing Feltham station on Sunday 29 April 2007.

Seen in Feltham on 29 April 2007, this is Travel London Dennis Dart RN52 EOB. Travel London was a subsidiary of National Express and was sold to NedRailways in 2009.

London United Leyland Lynx LX5 (G75 UYV) is seen at Hounslow bus station on Wednesday 20 November 1996. This was one of a very small number of Lynxes operated by London Buses.

Travel London Dennis Dart RN52 SPC passes Hounslow Heath on the 235 from Brentford to Sunbury Village on 5 February 2005. The 235 was created in 1996 to take over the western end of the 237.

Armchair Dennis Trident DT11 (KN52 NDO) is seen outside the famous Hussar pub opposite Hounslow Heath on Sunday 27 February 2005. By this time Armchair had been sold to ComfortDelGro (the owners of Metroline).

On 20 November 1996, London United Metrobus M195 (BYX 195V) is seen in Hounslow on the lengthy 237 from Sunbury to Shepherd's Bush, which has since been curtailed at its western end, running as far as Hounslow Heath. Most journeys on the 237 were operated at this time by all-Leyland Olympians.

Also passing through Hounslow town centre on the 237 is London United Metrobus M44 (WYW 44T), seen in June 1992.

London United Metrobus M179 (BYX 179V) is blinded for the 27, so presumably it must have run out of service from Richmond. It is seen at Hounslow bus station/garage on Sunday 1 September 1991.

Sunday 4 August 1991 sees Westlink Leyland National LS161 (THX 161S) and London United Metrobus M618 (KYO 618X) in Hounslow bus station. This was just before TGM started operating the 116.

London & Country Leyland National TOF 713S is seen at Bedfont Green, still in TGM livery, on Friday 21 August 1992.

TGM Buses Leyland National 3715 (TOF 317S) was looking very smart for its age when I took this photo at Bedfont Green on Sunday 1 September 1991. TGM had just taken over the operation of the 116 at this time.

London & Country Leyland National ERP 551T was still in TGM livery when seen in Bedfont Green on Friday 21 August 1992.

Midland Fox Leyland National BVP 821V is seen on hire to TGM at Bedfont Green on Sunday 29 September 1991. This bus later passed to Colchester Borough Transport.

The tender for the 116/117 was transferred in February 1992 to London & Country, which continued to use both its own Leyland Nationals and examples it inherited from TGM. NOE 598R is seen at the Bedfont Green terminus of the 116 on Saturday 11 December 1993.

London & Country Leyland National Greenway JCK 852W is seen in Hounslow on the 117 to Staines via Feltham on 24 June 1992. This was the very first National Greenway and it is now in preservation. Unlike a lot of National Greenways, this bus retained its original registration. When I saw this bus that day, I ran to take a photograph and I ended up slipping on the wet pavement and falling over. Thankfully I was able to recover in time to take this photograph.

London Buslines Leyland Olympian 47 (G47 XLO) at Hatton Cross on Wednesday 5 February 1992. London Buslines was a subsidiary of Q Drive and was sold to CenterWest in 1996. CenterWest was in turn taken over by FirstBus in 1997. This led to several of this batch of Olympians being transferred in later life to First Eastern Counties to be used on routes around Lowestoft and Great Yarmouth.

Seen in Hounslow town centre on Saturday 23 February 2008, this is Travel London Dennis Enviro 200 8748 (RN52 FRF), on the 235 to Sunbury.

Transdev Dennis Dart DP63 (T363 PRH) is seen in Hounslow on layover between duties on the 81 on Sunday 23 February 2008. At the time, the 81 was terminating in a street due to the redevelopment of Hounslow bus station.

By 2008 the 116 was operated using Transdev Dennis Darts. Single-door example DP3 (S303 MKH) is seen in Hounslow town centre on Sunday 24 February 2008.

Metroline Dennis Dart DP1007 (RX51 FNU) is seen at West Middlesex Hospital on 25 Monday 2008. Since the 117 was rerouted to this hospital it can only be worked by single-deckers due to a low bridge.

Taken at West Middlesex Hospital some five years later, on Wednesday 24 April 2013, this is Abello Dennis Enviro 200 8572 (YX61 BXG).

Transdev Dennis Dart DP42 (T342 PRH) is seen arriving into Hounslow town centre, nearing the end of its journey on the 222 from Uxbridge on Saturday 23 February 2008.

Transdev London United Dennis Trident TA205 (SN51 SYC) at Twickenham railway station on Wednesday 14 September 2011. London United has an interesting history since it was privatised, having changed ownership a couple of times, and has since reverted back to using the London United name after having spent some time under Transdev branding. Confused? I certainly am.

Abello Dennis Enviro 200 8508 (LJ08 CZR) is seen heading out of Twickenham on Saturday 14 September 2013.

London United Scania N94 SLE58 (YN55 NLJ) is seen in Twickenham town centre on Saturday 14 September 2013. Notice that after a period of wearing Transdev fleetnames this company had reverted to calling itself London United again. I'm the first to admit that I sometimes find it difficult to keep up with the changes to the ownership and branding of some of these companies.

19 November 1991 was a very dull, wet day in London. I seem to recall that it rained all day. A very wet London United Metrobus M1352 (C352 BUV) is seen on the 140 in west London, next to a very old (and equally wet) concrete bus stop. The flash from my camera is visible in the windscreen.

A Metroline MAN 11.190 with Optare bodywork, MV32 (N702 FLN) is seen in Southall on Monday 4 September 2000.

Also in Southall on that day was First CentreWest Dennis Trident TNL925 (W898 VLN). At the time a matter of months old, this bus was subsequently transferred within the First Group to Glasgow.

A First CenterWest Dennis Dart with fairly unusual Marshall bodywork, DML254 (S254 JLP) is seen at Ealing Hospital on 5 March 2000.

First CenterWest Metrobus M308 (BYX 308V) was passing Ealing Hospital on the same day on the trunk 207 from Uxbridge to Shepherd's Bush. This was about the time when the Metrobuses were being ousted from this route by the new Dennis Tridents. The 207 has seen an interesting variety of vehicle types over the years, including articulated buses. It was withdrawn between Hayes Bypass and Uxbridge in 2005, and extended to White City in 2008.

CenterWest Metrobus M389 (GYE 389W) is seen at Uxbridge Underground station, about to depart to Hounslow on the 222, on Friday 19 June 1992.

Luton & District all-Leyland Olympian LR82 (G282 UMJ) is seen in Uxbridge on 19 November 1991 on commercially operated service 348. These Olympians were a common sight in north London in the 1990s.

Atlas Bus Leyland Titan T357 (KYV 357X) is seen in Willesden on the 52 on Saturday 13 August 1994.

Taken from the pavement outside Willesden bus garage, this photo shows several Metroline double-deckers enjoying a day of rest in the early spring sunshine of Friday 3 March 1995. Note the shadow from the tree.

Above and below: On this page are a couple of images of Metroline Routemasters departing Willesden bus garage on Friday 3 March 1995: RML2566 (JJD 566D) and RML2698 (SMK 698F). I'm not sure if that tree was alive or dead when I took these photos but it has since been chopped down.

A very early Dennis Dart with Carlyle bodywork, DT93 (H93 MOB) of Metroline is seen at Kilburn Park station on Monday 6 February 1995.

Metroline Metrobus M1174 (B174 WUL) is seen arriving at Edgware bus station at lunchtime on the very sunny Friday 15 May 1998.

Friday 15 May 1998 was a very hot, sunny day. Seen on that day at Edgware bus station is Arriva London Metrobus M708 (KYV 708X). It is still in the livery that Cowie adopted for the Leaside business when it purchased it in 1994.

Also on 15 May 1998 at Edgware bus station is Metroline Dennis Dart/Plaxton Pointer EDR2 (M102 BLE). Behind is Luton & District Leyland Olympian G288 UMJ.

Metroline Dennis Trident TAL120 (X336 HLL) is seen in Neasden on Sunday 10 March 2002.

London Northern Scania N113/Alexander S5 F425 GWG is seen at High Barnet on Wednesday 13 September 1995.

Above and below: On this page are two photos I took of London Northern Metrobuses at the Friern Barnet town hall terminus of the trunk route 43 to London Bridge. M27 (WYW 27T) and M481 (GYE 481W) are seen on Friday 4 March 1994.

When London Buses was privatised in 1994, London Northern was sold to MTL, which in turn sold it on to Metroline in 1998. MTL London MAN 11.190 M508 ALP is seen here in Brent Cross shopping centre bus station on 3 July 1997.

On the same day Cowie Leaside Metrobus M548 (GYE 548W) is loading for the 102 to Edmonton Green.

Metroline Metrobus M1047 (A747 THV) is seen on 9 May 2003 at Brent Cross shopping centre in the distinctive livery with the deep blue skirt that Metroline adopted. By this time the Metrobuses were only on a handful of routes in London. The date stamp is incorrect.

Also taken on 9 May 2003 at Brent Cross was this photo of Metroline Dennis Lance L34 WLH. I do regret using the option of having the date imprinted on the image. But like so many things in life, it seemed like a good idea at the time.

Friday 29 July 1994 saw my one and only ever visit to Chase Farm. London Northern MCW Metrobus M1331 (C331 BUV) is seen awaiting departure on the W8 to the Picketts Lock Centre. The London Buses roundel had been removed by this point although London Northern was still part of London Buses and would be remain so until 26 October of that year, when it was purchased by MTL.

Armchair Leyland Atlantean GIL2603 (YKY 669T) was an ex-SYPTE/South Yorkshire's Transport vehicle. They had three of these Roe-bodied buses, YKY 669–671T (and three East Lancs-bodied buses, UDT 183–185S), all of which were reregistered with Northern Ireland plates and retrimmed internally. This photograph was taken at North Finchley bus station on Thursday 3 July 1997.

Leyland Olympian/Roe LR7 (TPD 117X) was new to London Country in St Albans in 1982. It later served at Hatfield, Ware and Harlow and survived into Arriva days. It is seen in Enfield bus station on Wednesday 11 December 1991.

Metroline Metrobus Enfield M1197 (B197 WUL) passing Enfield Town station on Wednesday 24 March 2004. This bus ended up as a clubhouse for a Scout group in Leicestershire – still in Metroline livery.

MTL London Metrobus M1143 (B143 WUL) and is captured along with an increasing rare Ford Cortina Mk 3 in a strangely quiet-looking road in Wood Green on 3 July 1997.

The old Turnpike Lane bus station is seen on Friday 4 March 1994. Leaside Metrobuses M614 (KYO 614X) and M919 (A919 SUL) are seen alongside an unidentified London Northern example. Soon the number of Metrobuses in London would start gradually dwindling, so scenes like this would quickly become a thing of the past. Turnpike Lane bus station was completely rebuilt a few years later.

Low-floor buses were still a bit of a novelty when I took this photo of Arriva London Scania N113 RDZ 1710 in Wood Green on 3 July 1997.

London Northern Metrobus M1330 (C330 BUV), seen in Wood Green on Monday 6 February 1995. Although London Northern was owned by MTL by this time, it had yet to receive the new fleetname.

Contrasting Metroline double-deckers on this page. Metrobus M1197 (B197 WUL) is seen on the left, right at the end of its life in London, on layover on the 317 (one of the very last London routes to have Metrobuses) while nearly new Dennis Trident TP429 (LK03 GFU) awaits its next turn on the 217. This is Waltham Cross on Wednesday 24 March 2004.

I couldn't resist taking this photo just a few minutes later as M1197 was being started up and belching out loads of smoke.

Metroline Metrobus M1076 (B76 WUL) was in a non-standard application of Metroline livery. It's also interesting to note that it was also devoid of fleetnames when I took this photo. This bus was a driver trainer that had been returned to passenger service, which probably explains these oddities as well as the camera on the front of the bus. It is on the 317 when seen on layover in Waltham Cross bus station on 16 February 2004. It was during this period that Metrobuses faded away from London service almost unnoticed while the Routemaster's gradual route-by-route withdrawal during 2004/05 received all the limelight and media attention.

For a long time several of Thamesway's Bristol VRTs soldiered on in outer London, still carrying Eastern National livery. In the fading light of Sunday 22 September 1991, 3089 (STW 33W) is seen on the 359. These low-height double-deckers were unpopular with the travelling public in north London, mainly due to the restricted headroom compared to the Metrobuses that they replaced on routes such as these.

Capital Citybus Leyland Olympian/Northern Counties 131 (J131 YRM) is seen at the bus station at Chingford railway station on Wednesday 27 November 1991.

Taken on the same day in Chingford and from the same fleet this is Dennis Dominator/Northern Counties 271 (H271 KVX).

County Dennis Dart J313 WHJ is seen at Chingford rail station on Friday 4 March 1994. This bus was later transferred to Arriva Cymru.

In August 2006 Stagecoach sold its London operations to Macquarie Bank, who restored the East London and Selkent names and logos. East London Dennis Trident 17809 (LX03 BXD) is seen at Chingford on Sunday 7 September 2008. In August 2010, East London, along with Selkent, was sold back to Stagecoach.

Cowie Group subsidiary Grey Green was predominately a coach operator that branched out into bus operation, winning several London Regional Transport route tenders. Metrobus Mk 1 466 (DTG 366V), new to Newport Transport, is seen at Chingford on Friday 4 March 1994, about to work the 179 to Barking.

A fairly unusual bus in the Grey Green fleet, this was a Scania N112 with East Lancs 'mock Alexander' bodywork, 113 (E113 KYN), seen at Chingford on 27 November 1991.

Arriva London DW448 (LJ61 CFL), a Wright Gemini 2-bodied VDL DB300, is seen passing along West Green Road, Tottenham, on 23 January 2015.

Go Ahead London General Volvo B9TL LK59 FDG is seen on Tottenham High Road on the 259 to Kings Cross on 23 January 2015.

A chance encounter on Tottenham High Road on 23 January 2015 saw Go Ahead Volvo B9TL WVN29 (LK59 FDP) and Bryans of Enfield former London General/Sullivan Buses Volvo Olympian NV122 (P922 RYO).

Arriva Wrightbus Gemini 2 DW454 (LJ61 CEY) and Go Ahead London General Volvo B9TL WVN13 (LK59 FEJ) are seen together in Tottenham High Road on 23 January 2015.

Cowie Leaside Metrobus M1370 (C370 BUV) has had its original upper-deck front windows replaced with non-opening ones when seen here on Tottenham High Road on 22 April 1997.

Cowie Leaside Metrobus M1165 (B165 WUL) is seen a few months later in Tottenham High Road on 12 September 1997.

London Suburban Buses was a subsidiary of MTL by the time I took this photo. Leyland Titan 516 T170 (CUL 170V) is seen at Tottenham Hale rail station on Friday 7 July 1995.

Leyland Titan 526 (formerly T202) (CUL 202V) is seen at Tottenham Hale, resting between duties on the 41 to Archway, on 7 July 1995.

When I visited Tottenham Hale on 7 July 1995, there were three different vehicle types being used on the 41 to Archway. Most journeys were being worked by Titans, but London Suburban Buses Volvo Olympian 201 (L201 SKD) is seen next to sister company London Northern Volvo Ailsa V1 (A101 SUU).

London Northern Volvo Ailsa V1 (A101 SUU) is also on the 41 when seen at Tottenham Hale on 7 July 1995. I recall that the driver had difficulty getting the bus to start and had to call the depot for advice on how to start it.

By 2001 the 41 was being operated by Arriva London. London Metrobus M1297 (B297 WUL) is seen on 9 May of that year at Tottenham Hale, looking a little bit unloved. The graffiti didn't help her appearance.

Arriva Wright Eclipse Gemini 2 LJ59 AEE at Tottenham Hale on 11 May 2015.

Above and below: On this page are two pictures taken on 7 July 1995 at Tottenham Hale showing Capital Citybus all-Leyland Olympians that were used on the 123 from 1991 to 1998: 154 (J154 YRM) and 155 (J155 YRM).

In one of two photos in this book taken by a friend of mine who joined me on a day out in London, Arriva Dennis Enviro 200 EN10 (LJ57 UTB) is seen at Tottenham Hale on Monday 24 June 2013. (Photo copyright Nigel Utting)

East London Leyland Titan T751 (OHV 751Y) is seen at Walthamstow on 28 November 1996.

Leaside Buses M613 (KYO 613X) is seen at Walthamstow bus station on Wednesday 13 September 1995. At the time Leaside Buses was a subsidiary of the Cowie Group, which would take over British Bus the following year.

Stagecoach East London Leyland Titan T579 (NUW 579Y) is seen departing the stands at Walthamstow bus station on 13 September 1995. It is curious that it still retains its white relief stripe a year into Stagecoach ownership.

The second photo taken on 19 November 1991. Thamesway Bristol VRT 3110 (XHK 15X) is seen at Walthamstow bus station on the 275. This bus later returned to the Eastern National fleet.

Capital Citybus Dennis Dominator/East Lancs 193 (F293 PTP) is seen at Walthamstow bus station on Sunday 21 July 1996. This bus was new to Southampton Citybus and saw further use in its later life with First South Yorkshire.

New to County in 1991, Arriva London Dennis Dart J309 WHJ is seen at Leyton Bakers Arms on Wednesday 9 May 2001.

Capital Citybus Leyland Olympian J141 YRM is seen at Walthamstow Bell Corner on 9 May 2001.

County Leyland Lynx H251 GEV is seen at Leytonstone on Sunday 21 July 1996.

Kentish Bus Leyland Lynx G39 VME is seen at Leytonstone on 23 December 1992. The following year the 108 was withdrawn north of Stratford.

Numerically the last Routemaster built, Stagecoach London Routemaster RML2760 (SMK 760F) is seen at Wanstead on a special working for charity on the 101 on Saturday 13 April 2013. While this bus was stopped at some traffic lights in Upton Park, a woman came up to the driver and asked if 'these are being brought back?'

Capital Citybus was sold to First in 1998 and subsequently integrated into First London. Dennis Trident TN860 (V860 HBY) is seen at Whipps Cross Roundabout on 9 May 2001.

Stagecoach East London Leyland Titan T517 (KYV 517X) is seen in East Ham on Wednesday 13 September 1995 in the all-over 'LT red' livery that Stagecoach adopted for East London and Selkent on purchasing them the previous year as part of the process of privatisation of London Buses.

Stagecoach East London T702 (OHV 702Y) is seen on 28 November 1996.

London Buses East London Leyland Titan T609 (NUW 609Y) is seen at North Woolwich on Wednesday 5 February 1992.

London Buses Leyland Titan OHV 686Y was originally numbered T686 in the London Transport fleet, passing to Stagecoach East London when London Buses was privatised in 1994. It was later transferred to Stagecoach Red & White, where it was numbered 811, before joining the Stagecoach in Lancaster fleet, where it received national fleetnumber 10686. It is seen in North Woolwich on Wednesday 5 February 1992.

When Stratford International station first opened in 2009, it was located adjacent to the construction sites of both the London Olympic Park and Westfield Stratford City shopping centre, which prevented pedestrian access. During local redevelopment work a temporary bus service linked Stratford International to nearby Stratford. The Docklands Light Railway station opened on 31 August 2011 and Westfield Stratford City opened on 13 September 2011. The bus service was discontinued on 20 September of that year. Go Ahead Dennis Dart/Plaxton Pointer LPD301 (R142 RLY) is seen on the temporary bus service on 11 July 2011.

Stagecoach London Scania N113/Northern Counties S34 (J134 HMT) was used on a Docklands Express service when new. It is seen in Stratford bus station on 19 June 1997. It would spend its final few years with Stagecoach in the East Kent fleet on services around Canterbury.

Capital Citybus 105 (JHE 138W) was an MCW Metrobus with a Rolls-Royce Eagle engine. It was new in 1981 as South Yorkshire PTE 1838. It is seen in Stratford bus station in the gloomy light of Wednesday 10 February 1999. It would later pass to Stevensons of Uttoxeter.

East Thames Buses was formed in 1999 to take over the services operated by the failed Harris Bus. It was then retained as an accredited operator to operate services in the event of the contracted operator being unable to do so. On 19 September 2002, East Thames Buses Optare Excel R376 DJN is seen in Stratford bus station. On 3 October 2009 Transport for London sold East Thames Buses to the Go Ahead Group, which incorporated it into London General.

Stagecoach Dennis Trident 17547 (LY02 DAW) is at London City Airport on Saturday 13 April 2013.

Go Ahead London General Dennis Dart LDP192 (SN51 UAE) is seen at London City Airport on Saturday 13 April 2013.

East London operated a number of DAF SB220s with Optare Delta bodywork in the early 1990s. DA14 (J714 CTG) is seen at the Claybury Broadway terminus of the since withdrawn 129 on Thursday 9 July 1992.

The revised 128 is essentially the same route as the withdrawn 129. On Monday 24 June 2013 Arriva Volvo B7TL VLA125 (LJ05 BJF) is seen at Claybury Broadway. (Photo copyright Nigel Utting)

Arriva Volvo B7TL VLA143 (LJ55 BTF) is seen at Gants Hill on 20 November 2013.

Arriva Volvo B7TLs VLA94 (LJ54 BDZ) and VLA143 (LJ55 BTF) are seen top and tail in Gants Hill on 20 November 2013.

East London Leyland Titan T15 (WYV 15T) is seen in Dagenham on Tuesday 11 May 1993. Behind is another early Titan. Both buses are carrying 'T' style adverts on their offsides.

Capital Citybus Dennis Dominator 348 (F148 MBC) is seen on 19 June 1997.

Devoid of the London Buses roundel, East London Leyland Titan T16 (WYV 16T) is seen on layover at Becontree Heath on 22 October 1994.

Almost two years later, at the same location but on a sunnier day, Sunday 21 July 1996, is Stagecoach East London Leyland Titan T4 (WYV 4T).

This photo of East London Leyland Titan T194 (CUL 194V) was taken from the pavement outside Barking bus garage in December 1991. At the time East London was part of London Buses and there was a lot of uncertainty regarding the future of London Buses, which very much hinged upon the result of the General Election the following spring.

East London Leyland Titan 573 (NUW 573Y) is looking smart in London Buses livery in Barking on Tuesday 11 May 1993. By the time I took this photo, it was known that the London Buses divisions would be sold during the lifetime of the current parliament.

Harris Bus Bristol VRT/Alexander PBD 43R is seen on rail replacement in Ilford on Sunday 27 February 1994. This was one of seven buses new to Northampton Transport that were sold to Harris Bus. The combination of the peaked upper-deck front bulkhead and rounded rear dome was unique to Bristol VRTs new to Northampton. This bus would be withdrawn and scrapped at the end of that year.

On the same day, a more modern double-decker from the Harris Bus fleet is also seen on rail replacement at the same location. Scania N113 F314 RHK was new to Harris Bus in 1989.

Rail replacement duties often have the effect of bringing out an interesting assortment of operators and vehicles. On Sunday 13 March 1994 Castle Point Daimler Fleetline GHV 43N, new to London Transport as DM1043, is seen loading in Ilford town centre.

Stagecoach East London Leyland Titan T471 (KYV 471X) is captured here in Ilford, coping in the slushy conditions of 2 January 1995.

Stagecoach London Dennis Dart 34202 (W202 DNO). This photo was taken on 1 May 2003.

Stagecoach Dennis Trident 17770 (LX03 BVF) is seen passing through Ilford town centre on the long and straight 86 from Romford to Stratford. In common with many long London routes, the 86 is significantly shorter than it has been in the past. This photo was taken on 1 May 2003.

First London Dennis Trident TN1058 (LN51 JGK) is arriving in Ilford town centre on 24 March 2004.

Arriva Volvo B7TL VLA130 (LJ05 GME) in Ilford on 14 May 2013.

Capital Citybus Volvo Olympian 167 (L888 YTT) was numerically the first Volvo Olympian to be built, on chassis No. 25001 (following the changeover from the Leyland designation). It is seen here when still quite new on Friday 29 July 1994. It is now part of the Bromley Bus Preservation Group collection.

Capital Citybus Volvo Olympian L888 TTT is seen at Ilford on Saturday 22 October 1994. Numerically, it was the second Volvo Olympian built, on chassis No. 25002. This bus saw further service with First West Yorkshire and it is also now preserved as part of the Bromley Bus Preservation Group.

Capital Citybus Metrobus UMS 751T is seen in Hornchurch on Monday 31 October 1994. One of only three to receive this style of body, it received the Olympian-style dash panel during its time in east London.

Capital Citybus Dennis Dominator 192 (F292 PTP) is seen in Hornchurch on Monday 24 January 2000. New to Southampton Citybus, sometime after Capital Citybus was sold to FirstGroup this bus was transferred to First South Yorkshire.

Stagecoach London Dennis Trident 17773 (LX03 BVJ) is seen between Seven Kings and Ilford in the London version of the 'rolling ball' livery introduced in autumn 2001. The date of this image is 1 May 2003.

East London Leyland Titan T14 (WYV 14T) is seen looking very smart in London Buses Limited livery in Chadwell Heath on 11 May 1993. By this time, of course, it was a matter of when not if London Buses was going to be privatised.

East London Leyland Titan T109 (CUL 109V) and Eastern National Bristol VRT 3092 (STW 36W) are seen in Romford in April 1990, just after Eastern National had been taken over by Badgerline Holdings. This Titan had to undergo extensive repair at Aldenham after it had been hit by an articulated lorry while working out of Barking garage in May 1986. The impact to the offside of the body was severe enough to push out the nearside. It was returned to service in February 1987 at Seven Kings. Sold to Merseybus in Liverpool in late 1992, it lasted until 2004 before being sold for scrap.

I took this rear view shot at the same time. It makes for an interesting comparison of these bus designs as it's easy to forget that both vehicle types were products of the Leyland Bus empire at the time. Indeed, the system for drawing in air to the engine through the offside grille and releasing it again through the grille on the nearside, so much a distinguishing feature of the VRT series 3, was derived from the development happening at the time on the Leyland B15, soon to be named the Titan. The difference in heights between the two types is apparent as well.

East London DAF SB220/Optare Delta DA15 (J715 CYG) is seen in Romford on the 129 to Claybury Broadway on Saturday 6 June 1992. This particular bus saw further use with Stagecoach South in the Winchester area and was reregistered YLG 332.

Capital Citybus Metrobus Mk 2 291 (F291 NHJ), still in Ensignbus livery, is seen in Romford on Saturday 6 June 1992. This was one of a large batch of Metrobuses purchased new by Ensignbus.

Capital Citybus Daimler Fleetline 227 (KUC 154P) is seen in Romford on 27 November 1991. By this time there weren't many Fleetlines left in the fleet. This bus was new to London Transport as DM1154. I was never any good at telling apart which Fleetlines had Park Royal bodies and which ones were bodied by MCW.

Also taken in Romford on that day, this photo shows Capital Citybus Dennis Dominator 253 (H253 KVX). This was one of a large batch of Dominators purchased new by Ensignbus not long before it sold its London Bus route operations to the CNT Group in December 1990.

County Leyland Lynx H256 GEV, with Townlink fleetnames, is seen in Romford between turns on the 66 on Wednesday 27 November 1991.

This photo was taken a couple of years later at the same location and not a lot seems to have changed, apart from the weather. County Leyland Lynx LX253 (H253 GEV) basks in the late winter (or early spring) sunshine on Friday 4 March 1994.

County Leyland Atlantean AN247 (KPJ 247W), wearing Thameside fleetnames, is seen in Romford on 27 November 1991 on the 373. The 370/373 between Romford and Grays was like a timewarp as these Atlanteans, new to London Country, were allocated to these routes for several years.

Blue Triangle Leyland National LN489 (TEL 489R), new to Hants & Dorset as 723, is seen at Romford Market on the lengthy 500 to Harlow on Sunday 4 August 1996.

East London Leyland Titan T34 (WYV 34T) is seen at Romford on 27 November 1991. These early Titans had long lives at Romford North Street bus garage.

A classic early 1990s view of Romford on Saturday 6 June 1992 with East London Leyland Titan T406 (KYV 406X) just arriving from Stratford on the 86, while County Leyland National SNB213 (LPB 213P) loads up at the bus stand. The Titan was later sold to Edward Thomas & Son while the National ended up in Yorkshire with a company called Big Foot. Note that the railway bridge is painted in the colours of Network SouthEast.

The first of its class, East London Leyland Titan T1 (THX 401S) is seen in Romford on a damp 26 May 1994. Not surprisingly, this vehicle is now preserved in its original livery, carrying the legend 'A New Leyland Titan for London Transport'.

Saturday 6 June 1992 sees two East London Leyland Titans on layover at Romford. T201 (CUL 201V) still has white-on-black number plates, while T213 (CUL 213V) has acquired reflective plates at some point. Both buses are on the 86. T201 has already been reset for Stratford while T213 still displays Romford.

East London Titan T642 (NUW 642Y) is seen n Romford on Friday 4 March 1994. After taking this photo I caught this bus, but it only made it as far as Seven Kings before breaking down.

East London Leyland Titan T545 (KYV 545X) on a damp Saturday 22 October 1994. This was around the time of the sale of East London to Stagecoach, hence the removal of the London Buses roundel.

Stagecoach East London Leyland Titan T633 (NUW 633Y) is departing Romford on the 87 to Barking on Sunday 21 July 1996. In 2006 the 87 would be withdrawn and replaced by an extension of the 5 from Becontree Heath to Romford. The number 87 was used to renumber the 77A, completing TFL's aim of discontinuing the usage of route suffix letters.

Looking resplendent in the all-over red livery Stagecoach adopted for its London operations (apart from the 'T' missing from its fleetnumber), T35 (WYV 35T) is seen in Romford on Tuesday 13 May 1997.

It's possibly a little surprising to see T40 (WYV 40T) still with the white stripe between its decks when seen in Romford on Sunday 21 July 1996. It is one of a number of Titans to now be preserved.

Previously with London Northern, Stagecoach East London Leyland Titan T578 (NUW 578Y) is seen in Romford town centre on Sunday 21 July 1996.

This photo was taken in the same location, but seven years later. Stagecoach London Dennis Trident 17293 (X293 NNO) later found itself in the Stagecoach Fife Scottish fleet. This photo was taken on 1 May 2003.

Also taken in Romford, but much more recently, on 20 November 2013, is this picture of Stagecoach Dennis Trident 17771 (LX03 BVG). This bus was sold to Applegate's Coaches.

Stagecoach London Dennis Trident 17507 (LX51 FNK) is seen in Romford on 20 November 2013. This bus was later transferred to Manchester and repainted into a blue Magic Bus livery.

Stagecoach Dennis Trident 17581 (LV52 HFO) is seen at Romford on 20 November 2013.

Arriva London Leyland Olympian G544 VBB is seen on Eastern Avenue on the 66 from Leyton to Romford on 1 May 2003. This is an unusual bus route in that a very large proportion of it is along an urban dual carriageway. This large batch of Olympians was new to Kentish Bus for the 22A/B and 55. The date on the image is incorrect.

New to Grey Green for the prestigious 24 in 1988, Volvo B10M Citybus F131 PHM is captured working on the 103 in Romford on a dull 7 February 2002.

Eastern National buses were for a long time a familiar sight in East London, particularly in Romford. Thamesway Leyland Lynx BN1424 (F424 MJN) (still in EN livery) is seen on layover at Romford station on Tuesday 25 February 1992 in the company of three East London Leyland Titans, including T80 and T142, about to work to Canvey Island via Brentwood and Basildon on the long-established 151.

Eastern National Leyland Lynx CF1429 (F429 MJN), numerically the last of the thirty Lynxes purchased by Eastern National in 1988, is at Romford station when seen on Saturday 6 June 1992, waiting to head to its home depot of Chelmsford. The 351 is a route that has changed many times over the years. Introduced in 1968, it worked all the way to Wood Green before being curtailed at Romford, then at Brentwood (Warley) before being reinstated to Romford. For a short while in the mid-1990s, it was extended from Chelmsford to Braintree. For about four months in 1999 it was briefly extended from Romford to West Thurrock. From Boxing Day 2005 it was once again curtailed at Brentwood as at the time First Essex had insufficient buses that complied with the emission regulations introduced by TfL. The new TfL route 498 was introduced at the time to replace the section between Romford and Brentwood.

It is difficult to believe that this photo was taken in Greater London. Historically part of Essex, Rainham has been in Greater London since 1965. On Tuesday 25 February 1992 Capital Citybus Metrobus Mk 2 280 (F280 NHJ) is seen in Rainham town centre at the start of its journey to Romford on the 103. Passing to First along with the Capital Citybus business, this bus later saw service with First Manchester.

East London Leyland Titan T545 (KYV 545X) appears for the second time in this book. It is seen in Noak Hill in the spring sunshine of 11 May 1993, looking very smart for an eleven-year-old bus.

Although quite a few miles outside of Greater London, I felt this photo was worth including as it shows a bus that would have normally been in use on the 193 in the Romford area at the time. This First Dennis Dart with Marshall bodywork, DMS41479 (LT02 NUV), is seen here stretching its legs on rail replacement at Shenfield rail station on 29 April 2007.

Although I've arranged the images in this book in a geographical order, starting with Bluewater and working my way around London roughly in a clockwise direction, finishing up in Shenfield, I've saved this image for last. On Saturday 14 May 2011, Routemaster RML2760 (SMK 760F), numerically the last Routemaster built, made a number of journeys for charity on the 5 between Romford and Barking. It is seen in Barking town centre on the afternoon of that day.